E
59
.A7
N4
1969

New York (City). Museum
of Modern Art

American sources of
modern art

DATE DUE			

AMERICAN SOURCES
OF MODERN ART

MAY 10 TO JUNE 30, 1933

THE MUSEUM OF MODERN ART
11 WEST 53RD STREET
NEW YORK

Reprint Edition, 1969
Published for The Museum of Modern Art
by Arno Press

THE EXHIBITION HAS BEEN SELECTED FROM THE FOLLOWING COLLECTIONS:

In addition to those who have lent works of art, the Trustees and the Staff wish to thank Mr. Horace H. F. Jayne, *Director of The University Museum;* Mr. Donald Scott, *Director of the Peabody Museum;* Mr. Edward Forbes, *Director of the Fogg Art Museum,* for assistance in assembling the exhibition; Dr. Clark Wissler, Dr. George C. Vaillant, Dr. Wendell C. Bennett, *of the American Museum of Natural History;* Dr. Alfred M. Tozzer, *of the Peabody Museum;* Dr. J. Alden Mason, *of The University Museum;* and Dr. Philip Ainsworth Means, for information and assistance; and Miss Dorothy C. Miller, for assistance in arranging the exhibition. The drawing on the cover is used through the courtesy of The University Museum, Philadelphia.

AMERICAN SOURCES OF MODERN ART

MODERN art, like everything else in modern culture, has a complex heritage. Among the diverse sources upon which it has drawn is the art of the ancient civilizations of America. The purpose of this exhibition has been to bring together examples of this art which are to be found in collections in the United States, and to show its relation to the work of modern artists. There is no intention here to insist that ancient American art is a major source of modern art. Nor is it intended to suggest that American artists should turn to it as the source of native expression. It is intended, simply, to show the high quality of ancient American art, and to indicate that its influence is present in modern art in the work of painters and sculptors some of whom have been unconscious of its influence, while others have accepted or sought it quite consciously.

The civilizations of ancient America have long been the study of historians and archaeologists but appreciation of the quality of their achievements in the arts is a comparatively recent development. After the first glowing accounts of the *conquistadores*, who were greatly impressed with the splendors of Mexico and Peru, very little enthusiasm was displayed for the works of American antiquity. From the time of the conquest up to the nineteenth century the usual reaction was one of wonder at the grotesque and colossal monuments of a people who, as Dr. William Robertson said in his history of America, were not entitled "to rank with the nations which merit the name of civilized." Dr. Robertson, who wrote in the latter half of the eighteenth century, was inclined to believe that the accounts of the *conquistadores* were the vapors of an overheated imagination. Against him one may set the opinion of another eighteenth century writer, the Abbé Clavigero. In his history of Mexico, Clavigero defends its ancient art against the attack of Dr. Robertson, and calls attention to the merit of certain works which he admired, though he too believed that they were not to be considered in the same category with the art of Europe.

Early in the nineteenth century the writings of Baron Alexander von Humboldt stimulated scientific and popular interest in the subject. In 1831 Lord Kingsborough began publishing his monumental work, *Antiquities of Mexico*, which included several rare texts and translations of early writers, and reproductions of some of the Mexican codices. Two American writers of the first half of the nineteenth century, William H. Prescott and John Lloyd Stephens, gave considerable impetus to popular interest in American antiquities in this country. Prescott's histories of the conquests of Mexico and Peru are well known to the American reading public. John Lloyd Stephens was a writer of great charm and a sensitive and discerning amateur of ancient American art who has been almost forgotten save by special students. Stephens explored the Maya region of Guatemala, Yucatan, and Chiapas in 1839 and 1842, and wrote two books about his expeditions. He took with him an English artist, Frederick Catherwood, who made what may be considered from the archaeologist's point of view the first trustworthy drawings of the architecture and sculpture of Copan, Uxmal, Palenque, Tulum, Labna, Chichen Itza, and other important Maya cities. In the narrative of his travels Stephens gives a just and accurate account of what he discovered and a graphic picture of these "once great and lovely cities, overturned, desolate, and lost." His first view of Copan convinced him that American antiquities were important "not only as the remains of an unknown people, but as works of art."

Our present knowledge of ancient American art and the specimens of it in museum collections we owe to archaeologists who began a systematic study of the material in the second half of the nineteenth century. Since about 1870, archaeologists, with the evidence of the spade, have more than confirmed the accounts of the *conquistadores* and the earlier writers. The research of the archaeologists, which has been made available to the general public in museum collections and illustrated books, has laid the foundation for a just evaluation of ancient American art. However, during the nineteenth century archaeologists found little general appreciation for the works of art which their spades uncovered. Since they were not primarily interested in esthetics they did not, in the face of public indifference, insist too much on the art quality of their discoveries.

During the past generation American antiquities have shared in the great development of interest in the art of exotic and primitive peoples. This interest, in its origins, was literary. It was one of the by-products of the romantic movement with its nostalgia for the exotic in time and space, for the art of past times and far-away countries. In the nineteenth century this romantic interest was focused largely upon certain periods in Europe's past and upon the arts of the East—Prosper Mérimée rediscovering French primitives, and the French romantics under the lead of Delacroix turning to the art of the Orient to deliver them from the Greeks and the Romans. The influence of the East is evident in the works of many nineteenth century artists, Delacroix, Whistler, Degas, Toulouse-Lautrec, Van Gogh, Gauguin. Toward the end of the century a turn toward the art of more primitive peoples was given by the South Sea pictures of Gauguin and the research of archaeologists.

It was not until the first decade of this century, however, that the art in the archaeological and ethnological collections began to make itself felt to any extent in Europe and America. At that time groups of young painters in Paris were inaugurating a period of experiments which in their audacity astonished the art world and which were to become the subject of heated discussion in Europe and America for many years. The standard bearers of this movement were the *Fauves* and the Cubists. In the light of their studies of Cézanne and of the Orientals and primitives these painters brought into the European tradition a renewed consciousness of the abstract qualities in art. In Hindu, Persian, Chinese, and Peruvian art they found suggestions for greater freedom and boldness in the treatment of color mass, and in African, Mexican, and other primitive and archaic art they found simplification of form, and methods for analyzing objects into design elements. About 1907 these painters discovered the art in the ethnological and archaeological collections of the Trocadéro. In 1908 came the retrospective exhibition of Paul Gauguin, and primitive art became a topic of excited discussion. Of the art in the Trocadéro, African sculpture had the most immediate effect upon the Cubist painters, but the Trocadéro's collections of Peruvian, Mexican, and Central American art were known to *Fauves* and Cubists alike. The cruder archaic type of Mexican and Central American art (Nos. 146-148) appears to have interested these artists most. However, they could not help noticing the combination of bold contrast and subtle color harmony in Peruvian textiles and feather mosaics, the powerful elemental construction and the tendency to formalism in the work of the Maya and Mexican sculptors and their solution of the problems of the relation of form and concept, realism and abstraction.

About 1909 American painters returning from Paris began to study collections of Mexican and Peruvian art in the American Museum of Natural History in New York. The earliest of these artists to turn to the inspiration of ancient American art was Max Weber. In Weber's *Cubist Poems*, published in London in 1913, there are several poems dedicated to works of Mexican art which he had seen in the Museum of Natural History. The Armory Show of 1913 intensified the interest in ancient American art among painters and sculptors, and one editor, Robert J. Coady, whose publication *The Soil* (1916-17), was one of the most important and original of the small magazines which have appeared in this country, devoted considerable space to this material. Such artists as Max Weber, William and Marguerite Zorach, Samuel Halpert, Ben Benn, and others were regular visitors at the Museum of Natural History during these years. Between 1913 and 1920, under the guidance of Dr. Clark Wissler, Dr. Herbert J. Spinden, the late Dr. Charles W. Mead, and M. D. C. Crawford, ancient American decorative motifs made themselves felt in contemporary arts and crafts through the work of a number of designers. Even before that time the influence of ancient Peruvian textile and ceramic design had been registered in German decorative art. In contemporary architecture the most distinguished student of the ancient Americans is Frank Lloyd Wright. Many architects, Major George Oakley Totten, Alfred C. Bossom, and others, have fallen under the spell of the great Maya and Peruvian builders.

In Latin America, of course, the influence of ancient American art has been present since the conquest. Native craftsmen and folk artists from colonial times preserved in their work something of their ancient tradition. A definite movement toward this tradition among the metropolitan artists began in Mexico in the early 1920's. An important figure in this movement was the anthropologist, Dr. Manuel Gamio. A call for a return to the native heritage of Mexico was sounded by David Alfaro Siqueiros in 1921, and by the founders of the Syndicate of Painters and Sculptors, which numbered among its members Siqueiros, Carlos Merida, Carlos Orozco Romero, Diego Rivera, Jean Charlot, and many other artists. "Let us", said Siqueiros, "observe the work of our ancient people, the Indian painters and sculptors (Mayas, Aztecs, Incas, etc.). Our nearness to them will enable us to assimilate the constructive vigor of their work. We can possess their synthetic energy without falling into lamentable archaeological reconstructions."* A similar return to ancient American art has been noted in Peru. Recently there has been a reaction against certain of these ideas, but it does not seem probable that the heritage of ancient American art will ever pass out of the consciousness of the artists of Mexico and Peru.

It will be seen that during the past thirty years ancient American art has come to be valued more justly by artists and art lovers. From an object of scientific investigation, exotic to the main stream of European civilization, it has come

*Translation by Anita Brenner in *Idols Behind Altars*, New York, 1929.

8

to be looked upon as one of the great arts of the world, a profound and original expression of the spirit of man which has much to offer contemporary culture. This changed point of view has led connoisseurs to make serious investigations into ancient American art for its own sake, and to study it with the same respect and care which they have applied to the study of the art of Europe and Asia. While the growth of popular appreciation has come about through the general interest in primitive peoples, ancient American art cannot, in its best periods, be called primitive. In such examples as the *Maize Goddess* (No. 37), *Lintel* No. 3, *Piedras Negras* (No. 67), *Stele* No. 13, *Piedras Negras* (No. 66), *Head and Torso, Copan* (No. 1), *Tiahuanaco Panel* (No. 222), *Feather-Mosaic* (No. 225), it is seen to be the art of high civilizations, though all these works were made with the implements of primitive man. This is one of the marvels of America's ancient civilizations, that they achieved an esthetic and scientific culture of a high order, a well developed agriculture which has given to the world several of its most important economic plants, and highly integrated and stable social and governmental organizations capable of carrying out immense programs of public works, all within the range of primitive technology.

The civilizations of Middle America and Peru did not know the use of iron. Their stone carving was done with implements of stone or of a low grade bronze. They did not know the mechanical use of the wheel, had no pulleys or derricks, and no draft animals (except the llama in Peru, which was used as a pack animal), but still they were able to cut and transport stones of enormous size. They did not know the true arch, or the potter's wheel, which was known to the earliest Egyptians. Their looms were extremely primitive. Yet within these practical and technological limitations they achieved a civilization which in many respects need not fear comparison with those of Egypt or Mesopotamia.

Behind the art of the Maya, the Mexicans, and the Peruvians was a diversity of cultures of primitive agricultural people called by archaeologists "archaic", out of which the high civilizations of America arose. Characteristic archaic products are terra cotta figurines and heads such as the group from the Museum of Natural History. Out of these archaic cultures, which date back several thousand years, rose in their turn the Maya of Guatemala, Honduras, Yucatan, and Chiapas, the Huaxtec and Totonac of Vera Cruz, the Zapotec and Mixtec of Oaxaca, the Toltec and Aztec of the Valley of Mexico, the Tarascan of Michoacan, and various other specialized cultures of Central America and Mexico.

The highest culture of ancient America was that of the Maya. Great as were

9

the achievements of this people in art and craftsmanship, their intellectual and scientific achievements were none the less impressive. Their mathematical and astronomical systems, their calendar which was the most nearly perfect in the world at the time of the Spanish conquest, their discovery of the concept of zero and place-value numeration which antedated the Asiatic discovery of the same concept by many centuries, and their development of hieroglyphic writing, must be numbered among the major achievements of mankind.

The Maya had already passed beyond the archaic level at the beginning of the Christian era. The earliest known Maya records, which date from the first century before Christ, show a well worked out hieroglyphic system which must have been perfected through centuries of development. At this time their sculptural and ceramic arts were already on a high plane, although their great period in sculpture and architecture comes a few centuries later. As builders the Maya show above everything else a feeling for mass and a genius for planning great architectural complexes. The relation between the architect and the sculptor must have been very close, possibly they were one and the same person, for this massive architecture is almost a form of sculpture. From certain technical points of view, such as the use of mortar and the keying-in of blocks, the Peruvians were their superiors as builders, but the Maya were excellent stone cutters and in the field of architectural sculpture the only thing that South America has to show which may in any way be compared with Maya art is the stone sculpture of Tiahuanaco. By the sixth century of our era the Maya had achieved a highly developed and perfectly controlled technique in stone carving. In such pieces as the *Maize Goddess* (No. 37) produced in this period, one realizes their extraordinary mastery of the carver's art, their sensitive modelling, and their fine sense of proportion.

There is high development and great stability of form in the products of Maya art as evidenced by a wealth of material from the known sites. Like the Egyptians, the Maya sculptors seldom carved the details of figures free, and sculpture in the round is not as common with them as carrying the relief around the block. Low relief is the usual mode of Maya sculpture. Even when the sculptor carved in the round his work is based fundamentally on a relief conception, probably because of the close relation between architecture and sculpture. The Maya sculptor was used to harmonizing his work with the surfaces of rectangular structures. He knew very well how to fill a given space and his arrangement is usually impeccable.

10

The highest development of sculpture in the round appears at Copan. (Nos. 38 to 42.) These sculptures date from the great period of the Maya, the height of which is placed by archaeologists at about the middle of the sixth century of our era.* In the seventh century Maya art declined. For some reason, unknown, the Maya abandoned their earlier sites of Piedras Negras, Copan, Quirigua, Tikal, Palenque, Uaxactun, etc., and migrated northward into Yucatan. Here, from the end of the tenth to the beginning of the thirteenth century A. D., there was a Maya renaissance which is associated with such cities as Uxmal, Mayapan, and Chichen Itza. In the thirteenth century began a period of Mexican dominance which appears to have centered about the cities of Mayapan and Chichen Itza. The destruction of Mayapan about the middle of the fifteenth century marks the virtual end of Maya civilization. The Spanish conquest in the sixteenth century did no more than mark *finis* to a great drama of civilization which had already been concluded.

In their sculpture, architecture, ceramics, and manuscripts the Maya left a coherent and unmistakable record of their civilization, and created ideals of form and a type of beauty which is entirely original and of a very high order. Formal ideals, such as those of the Maya, are not presented by nature. They are based on a great tradition in which standards have been evolved and perfected by countless generations of craftsmen.

For the modern taste the minus quality in the art of the Maya and other peoples of America, such as the Zapotec, is a fear of space, a tendency to over-design and to crowd detail. Maya artists worked in the service of an involved and ritualistic religion in which an all-important and elaborate symbolism led to tropical luxuriance of detail. These artists were trained to draw and carve a beautiful and intricate hieroglyphic system and this training, like the calligraphy of the Chinese, must have been a great influence in their work, tending on the one hand to masterly draughtsmanship and composition, and on the other to overcrowding. Even the vices of such great artists as the Maya have their virtues, and this overcrowding led to an amazing virtuosity in composing groups of interlaced figures and in the decorative use of line. Maya sculpture was originally painted in polychrome. Most of this painting has disappeared. In the known polychrome sculpture the color simplifies and clarifies the design, and mitigates the effect of overcrowding. For all its exuberance and profusion Maya art never loses its sense of architecture, its sound construction, and its monu-

*These dates are based on the correlations of Dr. Herbert J. Spinden.

mental quality. In such works as the *Maize Goddess* (No. 37), *Lintel No. 3, Piedras Negras* (No. 67), and *Head and Torso* (No. 1), there is a grand simplicity and a serene and austere beauty, sensitive and powerful modelling, and beautiful proportion. In figurines and small sculptures where religious symbolism was not all-important the Maya were capable of great simplicity of treatment. *Head of Figurine, Jonuta* (No. 134). In some of the carvings such as the jade heads (Nos. 52–57) one marvels at the technical virtuosity of artists who were able to carve extremely hard materials with stone tools and to achieve such delicacy and precision.

A feature of Maya sculpture and painting which has been noted by students is the solution of the problem of perspective. Perspective has been treated in a number of ways in various art traditions. The Maya handling of it is masterly. In the drawing of figures from any point of view they had developed conventions both subtle and precise. Their profile drawing in low relief sculpture, in pottery decoration, and in the codices shows a fine feeling for the abstract qualities of line—contour with them never deteriorates into mere outline.

A number of Maya frescoes of a late period have been discovered at certain sites like Tulum and Chichen Itza. Copies of some of these have been made by artists. (Nos. 240 and 249.) Our knowledge of Maya painting in its best periods is limited to ceramic decoration and to the codices, which are pictorial and hieroglyphic manuscripts painted and drawn on paper made from the maguey plant or on deerskin coated with a thin layer of stucco. Only three Maya codices are known to be in existence. The Maya painter, like the sculptor, was bound by ritualistic symbolism and convention, and this appears especially in the codices, which were records evidently dealing with astronomical and mathematical tables. The codices were written on a comparatively rare material and a great deal had to be crowded into a small space. The Maya pottery in this exhibition (Nos. 137–144) indicates something of the high quality of the work of these great artists, their clear conception of design, their sense of color, and of linear rhythm.

The art of the Toltecs and the Aztecs, tribes which were related to each other by blood and language, has less refinement than the Maya, but it has an elemental construction of great power. Because so much controversy surrounds the identification of the Toltecs, culturally and historically, the name "Toltec" is used here as a term covering the pre-Aztec Nahua peoples of the highlands of

Mexico. Writers like Charnay have postulated a great antiquity for this people, but in the light of recent research it appears that the rise of their characteristic culture took place during the first millenium of the Christian era and that their period of expansion began after the year 1000 A.D. They were an imperialistic people who embarked on a career of conquest a few centuries before the rise of the Aztecs. The great Toltec site is Teotihuacan, not far from Mexico City, and it is here that some of their best sculptures and frescoes have been discovered. The frescoes show that the Toltecs were daring colorists but that as draughtsmen they did not equal the Maya. Above everything else they had a sense of pattern. Their art is highly conventionalized in the direction of the decorative and the geometric, and shows a feeling for the dramatic. Toltec sculptures and paintings have a certain stiffness and angularity, but they are large in scale and have a monumental sturdiness (*Figure*, No. 94). A characteristic expression of the Toltecs is that of turquoise mosaic in which they produced splendid work. They were the great craftsmen of the later periods in the Valley of Mexico.

The Aztecs rose to power in the Valley of Mexico in the fourteenth century of our era, but the civilization which they assimilated was much older. Aztec sculpture has density and bulk, a powerful simplicity, and exhibits great skill in the cutting of hard materials. (*Aztec Jade Mask*, No. 59.) In their choice and handling of subject the Aztec artists had a tendency to the fierce, the macabre, and the terrible, and it is this quality which for a long time has stood in the way of popular appreciation of their art and which has at times thwarted such discerning critics as Elie Faure and Roger Fry. All Aztec art is not macabre or terrible in its imagery (*Girl's Figure*, No. 19, *Chalchihuitlicue*, No. 20) and its quality of fierceness gives it an intensity which enhances its esthetic value. Even such terrible conceptions as that of Coatlicue, the mother of the gods (original in Museo Nacional, Mexico City, casts at American Museum of Natural History, New York, and other museums) have an architectural and massive power. The ferocity of the Aztecs is never cold. It is passionate and human, just as their sacrificial rites were not an expression of mere cruelty but of a vivid sense of the awesome and overwhelming powers of the universe which man had to propitiate. They were intensely aware of the great forces of nature which could affect man for good or ill. Like the Maya they were astronomers, and this science, like everything else in their civilization, was an expression of religion. The priests and artists of Maya and Aztec alike communed with the stars, and events in the heavens assumed for them great dramatic importance.

13

Their art participated in the ceremonial drama of ensuring the benevolence of nature, and the continuity of life. It is this which gives ancient American art its intensity and sincerity, and which sometimes bows it down with a load of symbolic detail.

In the art of certain other peoples of ancient Mexico, the Totonacs, the Huaxtecs, and the Tarascan group of cultures, there is none of the Aztec ferocity or the tropical luxuriance of the Maya. The art of these peoples has much that makes a direct appeal to contemporary European and American taste. The Huaxtecs, who are considered a branch of primitive Maya, and the Totonacs approached the peak of their artistic development toward the end of the first millenium of our era. The Totonacs, on the evidence of the work which is ascribed to them, were gifted sculptors. Their technique in the cutting and polishing of hard stones was admirable. There is a combination of delicacy and strength in such carvings as the *Tattooed Mask* (No. 62) which is a mark of great art. The work of the Totonacs is less baroque than that of the Maya, and in general has more simplicity and grace, though it does not have its grandeur or imaginative power. Characteristic sculptures of the Totonacs are the beautifully carved stone "collars" or "sacrificial yokes" (No. 7), the pleasing and admirably modelled laughing heads (No. 100), and the so-called Totonac palmate stones (No. 8 and 9).

The art of the Huaxtecs is much closer to the archaic than that of their relatives, the Maya, whose influence they probably received through the Totonac. Huaxtec sculpture, like that of the Maya, is based on a relief conception. (*Figure of a Girl*, No. 11.) The modelling in this piece has an admirable simplicity and a certain refinement. The Tarascans evolved a highly characteristic style which is closer to the archaic than even that of the Huaxtecs. Possibly no other style has had more influence upon Mexican folk art and upon the professional artists who have been returning to the ancient traditions of American art. The art of the Tarascans is symbolic, but the symbolism is achieved, not so much through the massing and elaboration of detail, as through accent upon details which they considered significant. They were excellent craftsmen famed in Aztec times for their feather mosaics.

The art of the Zapotecs has a pleasing quality akin to that of the Totonacs, a quality which is not often found in the work of the sterner peoples of the Valley of Mexico. Their sculpture is primarily in the shape of pottery, though beautifully modelled stone heads and well carved jade ornaments are not uncommon. Zapotec art is decorative and runs to a geometric floridity in which decoration has a tendency to dissipate the form, but there is excellent modelling and a kind of monumental serenity. Their characteristic expression is that of profusely ornamented funerary urns (Nos. 149–150). They were great architects. Their architectural decoration at Mitla has the geometric regularity of textile patterns. The extant codices of Zapotec origin indicate that they were excellent draftsmen and colorists. As goldsmiths they were among the finest craftsmen of ancient America.

The decorative arts in the various cultures of Middle America attained a high development. Ancient American ceramic craftsmen did not know the use of the potter's wheel, but their best products, nevertheless, in beauty of proportion and decoration, have seldom been surpassed. Pottery in Mexico and Central America was made by the process of coiling and modelling, or it was cast in molds. No true glaze appears to have been known to these potters, but they were masters of slip painting and engraving. Paste and firing are usually very good. Maya pottery is distinguished by great subtlety of taste in decoration, with intricately composed groups of figures well placed in the decorative field, and a rich gamut of warm colors. The Toltecs were excellent potters and their sacred city of Cholula was still famous for its ceramics at the time of the Spanish conquest. (*Cholula Jar*, No. 119.) They show considerable development in range of color and technique such as that of an inlaid paste decoration not unlike cloisonné. They were mass producers of pottery heads and figurines, thousands of which have been found at Teotihuacan. The Zapotecs (No. 150), Miztecs (No. 102), Totonacs (No. 99), and Tarascans (No. 103) also were accomplished potters.

Maya sculpture, pottery painting, and codices indicate that from very early times they produced textiles and feather mosaics of great technical perfection. Their ceremonial costumes were intricate and beautiful in design, and were usually decorated with geometric patterns. The nature of the climate in the Maya area is such that these ancient textiles have disappeared. Wool was not known in Middle America but the Maya and the Mexicans both used cotton and various fibres which they dyed with cochineal, indigo, and several other dyes. The dress and personal ornament of the Aztecs have been described by Bernal Diaz.* He says: "When we arrived near to Mexico, where there were

*See bibliography.

15

some of the small towers, the Great Montezuma got down from his litter, and those great Caciques supported him with their arms beneath a marvellously rich canopy of green colored feathers with much gold and silver embroidery and with pearls and chalchihuites suspended from a sort of bordering, which was wonderful to look at. The Great Montezuma was richly attired according to his usage, and he was shod with sandals, the soles were of gold and the upper part adorned with precious stones. The four Chieftains who supported his arms were also richly clothed. . . ."

Of the decorative arts perhaps the most remarkable was that of the goldsmith. Writers of conquest times expressed great admiration for the gold work which they saw, and have recorded the fact that the goldsmiths of Seville despaired of imitating the products of Atzcapotzalco which was the center of the art in the Valley of Mexico in the Aztec period. Large quantities of worked gold are supposed to have been hoarded in the Aztec capital at the time of the conquest, but these disappeared very quickly. Excavation and dredging in Yucatan, Honduras, Costa Rica, Panama, Colombia, Ecuador, and Peru have brought to light much treasure of worked gold and silver. Various techniques were employed by the ancient American craftsmen, casting by the *cire perdue* process, smithing, a wire technique (Nos. 189–193), and work of great delicacy and beautiful design was produced by laying gold over pottery in a thin coat (No. 208).

As in every other complex of cultures which has been studied by anthropologists the art of ancient America shows an interchange of cultural elements between various centers of development. Any influence from outside the continent, above the level of primitive hunters, is improbable. The differences in the agriculture and technology of the Old World and the New up to the time of the Spanish conquest (the absence of the leading Old World food plants, large domestic animals, the wheel, iron tools, the potter's wheel, etc.) inclines archaeologists to the conclusion that ancient American civilization was entirely indigenous. The arts and the crafts of ancient America show a consistent development, as Dr. Herbert J. Spinden says, "within spaces of time that can be accurately measured and fixed in a system of world chronology." There is no evidence of a sudden break such as one might expect if the ancient Americans had come into contact with Old World culture, and such as did occur when they came into collision with it in the sixteenth century.

Earlier students have sought to find parallels for ancient American art in

Egypt and the Far East, and a cultural contact between these civilizations and America has been suggested. The coincidences of resemblance which have been cited to prove this cultural contact are not very convincing. The Americans built substructures for buildings which have been called pyramids. The similarity in name has led to the suggestion that the American builders got their ideas from the Egyptians, but Egyptian and American pyramids are alike in name only. The sculpture of such people as the Maya seldom has the symmetrical balance which gives a certain monotony to Egyptian art. In its asymmetry and occult balance it is closer to the Chinese, but this resemblance too is rather tenuous and cannot be condensed into the facts needed to prove cultural contact. These rather slight similarities were cause for marvel and conjecture among earlier students. However, as John L. Stephens points out, the fact that the arts of ancient America appear to be indigenous is "a conclusion far more interesting and wonderful than that of connecting the builders of these cities (Copan, etc.) with the Egyptians or any other people." The marvel, as he says, is the spectacle "of a people skilled in architecture, sculpture and drawing . . . and possessing the cultivation and refinement attendant upon them, not derived from the Old World, but originating and growing up here, without models or masters, having a distinct, separate, independent existence; like the plants and fruits of the soil, indigenous."

Recent writers on the civilizations of ancient Peru incline to the opinion that South America was peopled from Central America and Mexico by tribes which were already on the archaic level. They brought with them into South America a primitive agriculture, a rude architecture in adobe and wood, basketry, weaving, pottery making and other crafts. Since there was no written language in ancient Peru, precise dating is not easy and depends on archaeological evidence and on oral tradition which was put into writing after 1530. According to recent research* it appears that the earliest highland civilization, called by archaeologists Tiahuanaco I, rose out of the earlier archaic and ran its course in the Andean highlands between some unknown date B. C. and about 500 A. D. The most notable feature of Tiahuanaco I is its megalithic architecture. At about the same time there emerged on the Peruvian coast the cultures of Early Chimu in the north and Early Nazca in the south. The ruins of Chan-Chan,

*Dr. Philip Ainsworth Means to whose work this brief sketch of Peru is heavily indebted (see bibliography).

their capital, indicate that the Chimu people were architects and town planners on a magnificent scale. They were skilled craftsmen in weaving and metal working, and excellent potters (Nos. 160 and 161). Their art is predominantly realistic, though formalism is not entirely absent. The Chimu produced naturalistic portraits in pottery which are really sculpture, powerfully modelled and dramatic. (Nos. 111 and 160.) A marked sculptural sense is characteristic of Chimu pottery and of Peruvian pottery as a whole.

Contemporary with Early Chimu and possibly derived from it is the art of Early Nazca. The culture of this people is one of the most highly developed and interesting of ancient Peru. Its rise probably dates from the beginning of the Christian era. The Nazca people were the great colorists of Peru, and had a lively and imaginative sense of design. There is great variety of forms in Early Nazca pottery, and a wealth of decorative motives which run to the fantastic in combinations of demoniacal, human, and animal figures in designs which embody the myths of ancient Peru. A certain amount of realism may be found in Early Nazca design, but the spirit of the art tends to conventionalism and abstraction. The decoration is handled with the greatest freedom. The subject is distorted and dissected to suit the demands of symbolism and the nature of the decorative field. In Nazca art the influence of one technique upon another may be observed, especially that of weaving upon ceramic design. Early Nazca pottery is extremely well-fired. In technique, design, and color it was unsurpassed in ancient Peru (Nos. 107–110). Possibly the same may be said for Early Nazca textiles (Nos. 226 and 231) though it appears that the finest examples date from the period of Tiahuanaco II dominance.

The textile arts reached a high development in ancient Peru.* Peruvian ceramic products in modelling, beauty of decoration, and excellence of technique have rarely been surpassed, but the glory of ancient Peru is in her textiles. The Peruvian weavers produced many types of fabrics, tapestry, embroidery, brocade, gauze, pile fabrics, etc. With the exception of a few feather mosaics on a textile ground the finest work is probably in tapestry. In the best specimens the color is rich in bold contrasts or subtle harmonies with a great range of almost unnameable tints. Design is handled with sureness and freedom. The technique in spinning and weaving is excellent. The materials used are wool, cotton, and various plant fibres. No textiles from the period of Tiahuanaco I are known to be in existence, but many fine specimens from the Early Nazca culture have been

*Used as a term to denote the high civilizations of South America.

recovered from graves in the dry, sandy soil of the coast.

One of the best periods of ancient Peruvian textile art comes toward the end of the sixth century of our era. At that time the coastal cultures of Nazca and Chimu came into contact through trade, and probably also through war, with the highland culture of Tiahuanaco. The highland people were greatly stimulated by this contact, and the resulting development in their culture led to the civilization which archaeologists call Tiahuanaco II. The Tiahuanaco II style in textile design, pottery, and sculpture is highly individual. In the formation of this style the most powerful outside influence was probably that of Early Nazca. The tendency to convention and abstraction already present in the highly imaginative art of Nazca was developed by Tiahuanaco to an unprecedented degree. The style of the highland people runs to grandeur and solemnity as against the liveliness and dramatic sense of the coast. There is very little Tiahuanaco II pottery in American collections (No. 159), but there are many textiles of very high quality. Tiahuanaco textile design is controlled by a severe geometry. The color is rich and the technique excellent (No. 221–223).

The greatest works of monumental sculpture in ancient Peru, the megalithic sculptures and the great monolithic gateway of Tiahuanaco, were produced in the period of Tiahuanaco II. Massive architecture and sculpture in stone is confined largely to the highlands. In the coastal cultures the material for sculpture and architecture is clay. Peruvian sculpture, even the remarkable carvings of Tiahuanaco, does not have the intensity or feeling for form which characterizes the best work of Central America, but in the dressing and joining of large stones the Peruvians were supreme. The masons of Tiahuanaco II had a preference for large blocks of very hard stone which they finished and joined with meticulous care. Tiahuanaco II sculpture is characterized by block treatment, low relief, and severity and generalization of form.

The severity and restraint of the Tiahuanaco II style profoundly influenced the art of the coast peoples. The resulting development of esthetic ideas has given us some of the finest works of ancient Peruvian art. About the beginning of the seventh century of our era Tiahuanaco began a period of imperial expansion and for three centuries the style of Tiahuanaco II was dominant. It was a period of brilliant achievement in architecture, sculpture, ceramics, textiles, and in the working of metals. Such pieces as the superb *Tunic in Feather Mosaic* (No. 225) and the fine *Tapestry Fragment* (No. 222) were produced during this period.

19

In the ninth century, for reasons which may be inferred but have never been definitely established, the empire of Tiahuanaco II began to decline, artistically and politically, a decline which was complete before the end of the eleventh century of our era.

As the political and esthetic control of the highland culture relaxed the characteristic genius of the coastal people of Nazca and Chimu reasserted itself. Several dynasties appear to have flourished on the coast at this time. This section of Peru is cut up into mountain valleys. The art of Late Nazca is associated with the valley of Ica, where there was a new floresence of the imaginative and brilliantly colored pottery of Nazca. Late Nazca pottery decoration is not as vigorous and free as the earlier type, and runs largely to geometric patterns inspired by textile design, but there is a return to the old richness of color. The center of the Late Chimu culture was its ancient capital of Chan-Chan in the Moche Valley. In this region there was a return to the more realistic and dramatic art of the Early Chimu people, though the coast never completely shook off the influence of Tiahuanaco formalism. A characteristic ceramic product of this period is the burnished black ware with designs in relief (No. 175). There are many beautiful Nazca and Chimu textiles in this period, especially the kelim textiles, tapestries with slits (Nos. 228–229), and very interesting work in metal (Nos. 184–185).

In the twelfth century, the Incas, who were probably a small highland tribe, began their remarkable climb to power and embarked on an imperialistic enterprise which was not brought to an end until the third decade of the sixteenth century when they were conquered by the Spaniards. By 1400 A.D. the Incas had made good their mastery of a territory that spread out from what is now Peru and Bolivia to northern Ecuador and to northern Argentina and Chile. In art the Incas were eclectic, pursuing a mean between the formalism of Tiahuanaco and the livelier and more dramatic style of the coast. Essentially, however, their taste leaned to the more severe traditions of the highlands. Their art is not as subtle as that of the coast, but it does not run to the geometricizing which is characteristic of the later development of Tiahuanaco. There is clarity, harmony, and good proportion in Inca art, though it does not have the imaginative power, the color sense, or the subtle taste of its predecessors. Inca architecture, like all the architecture of ancient Peru, runs to grandeur. In pottery the characteristic Inca form is the aryballus which is admirable in proportion but does not equal the earlier pottery in modelling or in decoration (see No. 169). In the arts of the goldsmith and the silversmith there is much good work in the Inca period (Nos. 176–180).

The finest South American metal work in this exhibition comes from cultures which lie on the northern borders of the high civilizations of the Andean highlands, in Ecuador and Colombia. The Quimbaya (Nos. 195–201), were among the most famous of ancient American goldsmiths. In the ceremonial life of the Chibcha, gold had a large part. (Nos. 189–194). The high priest of the Chibcha, sprinkled with gold dust as he performed sacrifices at the sacred lake of Guatavita, was the El Dorado of the Spaniards.

Collections of ancient American art may be found in the museums which have lent for this exhibition, in the Brooklyn Museum, the Field Museum in Chicago, the University of California, and Tulane University in New Orleans, the national museums of Mexico, Guatemala, Peru, Costa Rica, Salvador, Colombia, Ecuador, and other Latin-American countries, the British Museum, the Trocadéro in Paris, the Museum für Völkerkunde in Berlin, the Linden Museum in Stuttgart, the Kircheriano in Rome, The Naturhistoriches Museum in Vienna, the Museum für Völkerkunde in Munich, and museums in Hamburg, Madrid, Liverpool, and various other European cities.

Since 1927 the Fogg Museum in Cambridge has devoted one of its galleries to Maya art loaned by the Peabody Museum. In 1928 there was an exhibition under the auspices of the Musée des Arts Decoratifs in Paris. In 1931 a fine exhibition of Middle American and Peruvian art was shown at the Century Club in New York. In 1932 the state museums of Berlin and the Ibero-American Institute sponsored an exhibition which was shown at the Berlin Academy.

HOLGER CAHILL

BIBLIOGRAPHY

ALEXANDER, H. B., *Latin-American Mythology*. Boston, 1920

BAESSLER, ARTHUR, *Ancient Peruvian Art*. Translated by A. H. Keane. 4 vols. Berlin and New York, 1902–03

BANDELIER, A. F., *On the Art of War and Mode of Warfare of the Ancient Mexicans; On the Distribution and Tenure of Land, and the Customs with Respect to Inheritance, among the Ancient Mexicans; On the Social Organization and Mode of Government of the Ancient Mexicans*. Peabody Museum, Annual Reports, vol. II. Cambridge, Mass., 1877–80

———— *Report of an Archaeological Tour in Mexico in 1881*. Archaeological Institute of America, Papers, American Series, II. Boston, 1881

BASLER, ADOLPHE *and* BRUMMER, ERNEST, *L'Art Précolumbien*. Paris, 1928

BATRES, LEOPOLDO, *Exploraciones de Monte Alban*. Mexico, 1902

BEUCHAT, HENRI, *Manuel d'Archéologie Américaine*. Paris, 1912

BRASSEUR DE BOURBOURG, C. E., *Histoire des Nations Civilisées du Mexique et de l'Amérique Centrale durant les Siècles Antérieurs à Christophe Colomb*. 4 vols. Paris, 1857–59

BRINTON, D. G., *The Maya Chronicles*. Philadelphia, 1882

CASO, ALFONSO, *Reading the Riddle of Ancient Jewels. An Analysis of the Historical Significance of the Monte Alban Treasure*. Natural History, XXXII, 5. New York, 1932

CATHERWOOD, FREDERICK, *Views of Ancient Monuments in Central America, Chiapas and Yucatan*. London, 1844

CHARNAY, DESIRÉ, *The Ancient Cities of the New World*. Translated by J. Gonino and H. S. Conant. London, 1887

CLAVIGERO, F. S., *The History of Mexico*. Translated by Charles Cullen. 2 vols. London, 1787

CODICES

Some of the codices which are most interesting from the point of view of art are listed here. Several codices will also be found in Kingsborough and Peñafiel.

Aubin-Goupil collection of pre-Columbian and post-Columbian codices and maps in National Library, Paris. Published by E. Boban, Paris, 1891

Codex Borbonicus, a pre-Columbian codex in Library of the Chamber of Deputies, Paris. Published by Leroux with commentary by E. T. Hamy, Paris, 1899

Codex Borgianus, a pre-Columbian codex in Ethnographical Museum of the Vatican, Rome. Published by Duc de Loubat, Rome, 1898, and by E. Seler, Berlin, 1904–09

Codex Cospianus, a pre-Columbian codex in library of University of Bologna. Published by Duc de Loubat, Rome, 1898

Codex Dresden, a pre-Columbian Maya codex in Dresden Library. Published by E. Förstemann, Leipzig, 1880 and 1892

Codex Fejérváry-Mayer, a pre-Columbian codex in Free Public Museums, Liverpool. Published by Duc de Loubat with commentary by E. Seler, Berlin, 1901

Codex Telleriano-Remensis, a post-Columbian codex in National Library, Paris. Published by Duc de Loubat with commentary by E. T. Hamy, Paris, 1899

Codex Tro-Cortesianus, a pre-Columbian Maya codex in two halves in National Archaeological Museum, Madrid. Published by Leon de Rosny, Paris, 1883 (Cortesianus), and by Brasseur de Bourbourg, Paris, 1869–70 (Troano)

Codex Vaticanus B (3773), a pre-Columbian codex in Vatican Library, Rome. Published by Duc de Loubat with commentary by E. Seler, Berlin, 1902–03

Codex Vienna, a pre-Columbian codex in National Library, Vienna. Published by M. Jaffé with commentary by W. Lehmann and O. Smital, Vienna, 1929

Codex Zouche (Nuttall), a pre-Columbian codex found in a private library in England, now in British Museum. Published by Peabody Museum with commentary by Z. Nuttall, Cambridge, Mass., 1902

DANZEL, TH. W., *Mexiko I: Grundzüge der Altmexikanischen Geisteskultur; Mexiko II: Kultur und Leben im Alten Mexiko.* (Kulturen der Erde.) Hagen and Darmstadt, 1922

DIAZ DEL CASTILLO, BERNAL, *The True History of the Conquest of Mexico, 1568.* Translated by A. P. Maudslay. 5 vols. London, 1908–16

DIESELDORFF, E. P., *Kunst und Religion der Maya-Völker im Alten und Heutigen Mittelamerika.* 3 vols. Berlin, 1926, 1931 and 1933

DUPAIX, GUILLELMO, *Antiquités Mexicaines. Relation des trois expéditions du Capitaine Dupaix, ordonnées en 1805, 1806, et 1807 . . .* Paris, 1834–36

FUHRMANN, ERNEST, *Mexiko III: Über die Religiösen Kulte im dem Alten Mexiko; (Peru I): Reich der Inka; Peru II.* (Kulturen der Erde.) Hagen and Darmstadt, 1922

GAMIO, MANUEL, *La Poblacion del Valle de Teotihuacan.* 2 vols. Mexico, 1922

GANN, T. W. F., *Mounds in Northern British Honduras*. Bureau of American Ethnology, 19th Annual Report. Washington, 1898

———— *The Maya Indians of Southern Yucatan and Northern British Honduras*. Bureau of American Ethnology, Bulletin 64. Washington, 1918

———— and THOMPSON, J. E., *The History of the Maya from the Earliest Times to the Present Day*. New York, 1931

GARCILASO DE LA VEGA, *First Part of the Royal Commentaries of the Yncas*. Translated and edited by C. R. Markham. London, 1869–71

GORDON, G. B., *Examples of Maya Pottery in the Museum and Other Collections*. 2 parts. Pennsylvania University Museum. Philadelphia, 1925

HABEL, SIMEON, *The Sculptures of Santa Lucia Cosumalwhuapa in Guatemala*. Smithsonian Contributions to Knowledge. Washington, 1878

HAMY, E. T., *Galerie Américaine du Musée d'Ethnographie du Trocadéro*. 2 parts. Paris, 1897

HARCOURT, RAOUL D' and M. D', *La Céramique Ancienne du Pérou*. Paris, 1924

———— *Les Tissus Indiens du Vieux Pérou*. Paris, 1924

HARTMAN, C. V., *Archaeological Researches in Costa Rica*. The Royal Ethnographical Museum in Stockholm. Stockholm, 1901

HOLMES, W. H., *Archaeological Studies amongst the Ancient Cities of Mexico*. Field Museum of Natural History. Chicago, 1895–97

HUMBOLDT, ALEXANDER VON, *Vues des Cordillères et Monumens des Peuples Indigènes de l'Amérique*. Paris, 1810

JOYCE, T. A., *Central American and West Indian Archaeology*. New York, 1916

———— *Maya and Mexican Art*. London, 1927

———— *Mexican Archaeology*. London and New York, 1912

———— *South American Archaeology*. London and New York, 1912

KINGSBOROUGH, LORD, *Antiquities of Mexico*. 9 vols. London, 1831–48

LANDA, DIEGO DE, *Relacion de las Cosas de Yucatan*. Edited with French translation by Brasseur de Bourbourg. Paris, 1864

Lehmann, Walter, *Zentral-Amerika*. 2 vols. Berlin, 1920

———— and Doering, Heinrich, *The Art of Old Peru*. London and New York, 1924

Lothrop, S. K., *Pottery of Costa Rica and Nicaragua*. 2 vols. Museum of the American Indian, Heye Foundation. New York, 1926

———— *Tulum; an archaeological study of the east coast of Yucatan*. Carnegie Institution. Washington, 1924

Lumholtz, Carl, *Unknown Mexico*. 2 vols. New York, 1902

MacCurdy, G. G., *A Study of Chiriquian Antiquities*. Connecticut Academy of Arts and Sciences, Memoirs, III. New Haven, 1911

Mariscal, F. E., *Estudio Arquitectonico de las Ruinas Mayas, Yucatan y Campeche*. Contribucion de Mexico al XXIII Congreso de Americanistas. Mexico, 1928

Markham, C. R., *The Incas of Peru*. London, 1910

Marquina, Ignacio, *Estudio Arquitectonico Comparativo de los Monumentos Arqueologicos de Mexico*. Contribucion de Mexico al XXIII Congreso de Americanistas. Mexico, 1928

Mason, J. A., *What We Know about the Maya*. Pennsylvania University Museum, Journal, XVIII. Philadelphia, 1927

Maudslay, A. P., *Biologia Centrali-Americana. Archaeology*. 4 vols. London, 1889–1902

Means, P. A., *Ancient Civilizations of the Andes*. New York and London, 1931

———— *Peruvian Textiles. Examples of the Pre-Incaic Period*. Introduction by Joseph Breck. Metropolitan Museum of Art. New York, 1930

Mexican and Central American Antiquities, Calendar Systems, and History. Twenty-four papers by Eduard Seler, E. Förstemann, Paul Schellhas, Carl Sapper, and E. P. Dieseldorff. Bureau of American Ethnology, Bulletin 28. Washington, 1904

Morley, S. G., *An Introduction to the Study of the Maya Hieroglyphs*. Bureau of American Ethnology, Bulletin 57. Washington, 1915

———— *The Inscriptions at Copan*. Carnegie Institution. Washington, 1920

Morris, E. H., Charlot, Jean and Morris, A. A., *The Temple of the Warriors at Chichen Itza, Yucatan*. 2 vols., Carnegie Institution. Washington, 1931

Nuttall, Zelia, *The Island of Sacrificios*. American Anthropologist, New Series, XII. Lancaster, Pa., 1910

Peabody Museum of Harvard University. Memoirs I–VI. (Reports on excavations and exploration by G. B. Gordon, Teobert Maler, R. E. Merwin, H. J. Spinden, E. H. Thompson, A. M. Tozzer and G. C. Vaillant)

Peñafiel, Antonio, *Monumentos del Arte Mexicano Antiguo*. 3 vols. in 5. Berlin, 1890

Prescott, W. H., *History of the Conquest of Mexico*. 3 vols. New York, 1843. Also edition illustrated by Keith Henderson, London, 1922

——— *History of the Conquest of Peru*. 2 vols. New York, 1847

Preuss, K. Th., *Monumentale vorgeschichtliche Kunst*. 2 vols. Göttingen, 1929

Reiss, Wilhelm and Stübel, Alphons, *The Necropolis of Ancon in Peru*. Translated by A. H. Keane. 3 vols. Berlin, 1880–87

Sahagun, Bernardino de, *Histoire générale des choses de la Nouvelle-Espagne*. Edited and translated by D. Jourdanet and R. Siméon. Paris, 1880. Also an edition in English translated by Fanny R. Bandelier. Nashville, Tenn., 1932

The Sahagun Codex, a series of post-Columbian paintings accompanying the Nahuatl text of Sahagun's *Historia General de las Cosas de Nueva España*, edited by Francisco del Paso y Troncoso. Vols. V–VIII. Madrid, 1905–07

Saville, M. H., *The Antiquities of Manabi, Ecuador*. 2 vols. Museum of the American Indian, Heye Foundation. New York, 1907–10

——— *The Goldsmith's Art in Ancient Mexico*. Museum of the American Indian, Heye Foundation. New York, 1920

——— *The Wood Carver's Art in Ancient Mexico*. Museum of the American Indian, Heye Foundation. New York, 1925

——— *Turquois Mosaic Art in Ancient Mexico*. Museum of the American Indian, Heye Foundation. New York, 1922

Schellhas, Paul, *Representation of Deities of the Maya Manuscripts*. Second edition revised, translated by Selma Wesselhoeft and A. M. Parker. Peabody Museum, Papers, IV, 1. Cambridge, Mass., 1904

Schmidt, Max, *Kunst und Kultur von Peru*. Berlin, 1929

SELER, EDUARD, *Gesammelte Abhandlungen zur Amerikanischen Sprach- und Alterthumskunde.* 5 vols. Berlin, 1902–23

SPINDEN, H. J., *Ancient Civilizations of Mexico and Central America.* Third edition. American Museum of Natural History. New York, 1928

———— *A Study of Maya Art.* Peabody Museum, Memoirs, VI. Cambridge, Mass., 1913

———— *The Reduction of Maya Dates.* Peabody Museum, Papers, VI, 4. Cambridge, Mass., 1924

STEPHENS, J. L., *Incidents of Travel in Central America, Chiapas, and Yucatan.* 2 vols., illustrated by Frederick Catherwood. New York, 1841

———— *Incidents of Travel in Yucatan.* 2 vols., illustrated by Frederick Catherwood. New York, 1843

STREBEL, HERMANN, *Alt Mexiko. Archäologische Beiträge zur Kulturgeschichte seiner Bewohner.* 2 vols. Hamburg and Leipzig, 1885–89

———— *Ueber Ornamente auf Tongefässen aus Alt-Mexiko.* Hamburg and Leipzig, 1904

STÜBEL, ALFONS and UHLE, MAX, *Die Ruinenstaette von Tiahuanaco im Hochlande des Alten Peru.* Breslau, 1892

TELLO, J. C., *Introducción a la Historia Antigua del Perú.* Lima, 1921

————, editor, *Wira Kocha; Revista Peruana de Estudios Antropologicos.* Vol. I. Lima, 1931

THOMPSON, J. E., *Mexico before Cortes.* New York, 1933

————, POLLOCK, H. E. D. and CHARLOT, JEAN, *Preliminary Study of the Ruins of Cobá, Quintana Roo, Mexico.* Carnegie Institution. Washington, 1932

TOTTEN, G. O., *Maya Architecture.* Washington, 1926

UHLE, MAX, *Kultur und Industrie Südamerikanischer Völker.* 2 vols. Berlin, 1889–90

———— *Pachacamac.* University of Pennsylvania, Department of Archaeology. Philadelphia, 1903

VAILLANT, G. C., *Excavations at Zacatenco; Excavations at Ticoman.* American Museum of Natural History, Anthropological Papers, XXXII, 1–2. New York, 1930–31

WALDECK, J. F. DE, *Monuments anciens du Mexique.* With introduction by Brasseur de Bourbourg. Paris, 1866

———— *Voyage Pittoresque et Archéologique dans la Province de Yucatan pendant 1834 et 1836.* Paris, 1838

CATALOG

An asterisk before a catalog number indicates that the work is illustrated by a plate bearing the same number.

SCULPTURE

Lent by the American Museum of Natural History, New York

1 HEAD AND TORSO OF SINGING FIGURE
Maya culture. Copan, Honduras

2 LONG TOOTHED GOD (of rain?)
Maya culture. Copan, Honduras

3 HEAD, architectural detail
Late Maya culture. Uxmal, Yucatan
Collected by J. L. Stephens

John Lloyd Stephens (1805–1852) was a graduate of Columbia University, an engineer, and an organizer and builder of railroad and steamship lines. Among his achievements was the building of the first railroad across the Isthmus of Panama. In 1839 President Van Buren sent him to negotiate a treaty with the Central American Republic. At that time the Republic was going through the revolution which led to the formation of the present Central American states, and Stephens, unable to accomplish his diplomatic mission, devoted himself to exploration and study of the Maya ruins. Stephens at one time bought the ruins of Copan for fifty dollars! He intended to transport its monuments to New York and to use them as the nucleus for a great national museum. This project, of course, was never realized, but Stephens did bring back from Yucatan a collection of sculpture and pottery which he placed on exhibition in New York. The pottery and some of the sculptures were destroyed in a fire, but several pieces which had not arrived from Yucatan when the fire occurred, and of which this is one, are now owned by the American Museum of Natural History.

*4 STONE MASK
Totonac culture. Vera Cruz, Mexico

*5 STONE DISK (mirror?)
Totonac culture. Vera Cruz, Mexico

6 FIGURE IN SERPENTINE WITH SHELL INLAY
Probably Totonac culture. Vera Cruz, Mexico

*7 STONE YOKE USED IN EXPIATORY CEREMONIES
Totonac culture. Vera Cruz, Mexico

8 PALMATE STONE WITH RELIEF SHOWING CEREMONIAL SCENE
Totonac culture. Vera Cruz, Mexico

9 PALMATE STONE WITH TURKEY
Totonac culture. Vera Cruz, Mexico (Stone is shown in reverse)

10 STONE MASK
Late "Toltec" culture. Puebla, Mexico

*11 SEATED FIGURE OF YOUNG GIRL
Late Huaxtec culture. Northern Vera Cruz, Mexico

12 HEAD
Olmec (?) culture. Vera Cruz, Mexico

*13 STONE FIGURE OF TATTOOED MAN
Guetar culture. Costa Rica

14 PROFILE HEAD
Mixtec (?) culture. Mistequilla, Oaxaca, Mexico

15 MONKEY HEAD
Culture unknown. Guerrero, Mexico

16 MONKEY HEAD
Culture unknown. Guerrero, Mexico

17 CONVENTIONALIZED MASK
Culture unknown. Mazela, Guerrero, Mexico

18 CONVENTIONALIZED MASK
San Miguel, Guerrero, Mexico

*19 FIGURE OF YOUNG GIRL (Maize Goddess)
Aztec culture. Valley of Mexico

*20 GODDESS CHALCHIHUITLICUE
Aztec culture. Valley of Mexico

*21 TWO-TONED DRUM OF WOOD IN FORM OF TIGER
Aztec culture. Valley of Mexico

22 JADE CARVING
   Maya (?) culture. Ococingo, Chiapas, Mexico

23 JADE CARVING
   Maya (?) culture. Ococingo, Chiapas, Mexico

24 JADE CARVING
   Maya (?) culture. Ococingo, Chiapas, Mexico

Lent by the Museum of the American Indian, Heye Foundation, New York

25 STONE HEAD
   Maya culture. Quirigua, Guatemala

*26 STONE HEAD, architectural ornament
   Maya culture. Copan, Honduras

27 IDOL IN GREEN STONE
   Maya culture. Copan, Honduras

28 JADE ORNAMENT WITH FIGURE OF SEATED PRIEST

29 JADE ORNAMENT WITH SEATED FIGURE WITH ANIMAL MASK
   Oaxaca, Mexico

*30 GOD XIPE TOTEC, "the flayed one"
   Aztec culture. Pepepan, Valley of Mexico. *This piece is dated 1507 A.D.*

*31 SEATED STONE FIGURE
   San Bartolo, Mexico

32 HUMAN HEAD OF OBSIDIAN
   Valley of Mexico

33 ALABASTER MASK
   Valley of Mexico

34 ONYX MASK
   Valley of Mexico

31

*35 STANDING FIGURE IN GREEN STONE
Central Mexico

*36 STONE CARVING REPRESENTING ANIMAL HEAD
Chilanga, Salvador

Lent by the Peabody Museum of Harvard University, Cambridge, Massachusetts

*37 HEAD OF MAIZE GODDESS IN TRACHYTE, facade ornament
Maya culture. Copan, Honduras. *About 515 A.D.*

38 HEAD OF MAIZE GODDESS IN TRACHYTE, showing remains of paint. Facade ornament. *Maya culture.* Copan, Honduras. *About 515 A.D.*

39 PORTION OF FIGURE IN TRACHYTE, facade ornament
Maya culture. From debris near western wall of Temple 22, Copan, Honduras. *About 525 A.D.*

40 LOWER PART OF FIGURE IN TRACHYTE
Maya culture. From Temple 22, Copan, Honduras. *About 525 A.D.*

*41 SERPENT HEAD IN TRACHYTE, probably a corner ornament on a temple
Maya culture. From Temple 21, Copan, Honduras. *About 525 A.D.*

42 GROTESQUE HEAD IN TRACHYTE, facade ornament
Maya culture. Copan, Honduras. *About 525 A.D.*

*43 ROMAN NOSED GOD IN TRACHYTE
Maya culture. From hieroglyphic stairway, Copan, Honduras. *About 450 A.D.*

44 FEATHER DESIGN IN TRACHYTE, facade ornament
Maya culture. Copan, Honduras. *About 500 A.D.*

*45 LINTEL NO. 2, PIEDRAS NEGRAS, GUATEMALA
Maya culture. The hieroglyphic inscription gives the Maya date 9.11.6.2.1. (398 A.D.)

*46 PORTION OF LINTEL NO. 1 IN LIMESTONE, PIEDRAS NEGRAS, GUATEMALA
Maya culture. Approximately the same date as Lintel No. 2

*47 HEAD OF A GOD IN STUCCO
Maya culture. Palenque, Chiapas, Mexico. (Stucco was used extensively in place of stone carving at Palenque.)

32

48 SQUARE JADE PLAQUE, PALENQUE TYPE
Maya culture. From Cenote of Sacrifice, Chichen Itza, Yucatan

49 CIRCULAR JADE PLAQUE, PALENQUE TYPE
Maya culture. From Cenote of Sacrifice, Chichen Itza, Yucatan

*50 PORTION OF JADE AMULET, PIEDRAS NEGRAS TYPE
Maya culture. From Cenote of Sacrifice, Chichen Itza, Yucatan

51 JADE NECKLACE AND HEAD (assembled)
Maya culture. From Cenote of Sacrifice, Chichen Itza, Yucatan. (Note similarity to necklace in No. 39.)

*52 HEAD IN JADE
Maya culture. From Cenote of Sacrifice, Chichen Itza, Yucatan

*53 HEAD IN JADE
Maya culture. From Cenote of Sacrifice, Chichen Itza, Yucatan

*54 HEAD IN JADE
Maya culture. From Cenote of Sacrifice, Chichen Itza, Yucatan

*55 HEAD IN JADE
Maya culture. From Cenote of Sacrifice, Chichen Itza, Yucatan

*56 HEAD IN JADE
Maya culture. From Cenote of Sacrifice, Chichen Itza, Yucatan

*57 SMALL RELIEF IN JADE
Maya culture. From Cenote of Sacrifice, Chichen Itza, Yucatan

58 LARGE SERPENTINE MASK
Aztec culture. Mexico

*59 JADE MASK REPRESENTING GODDESS COYALXANHIU
Aztec culture. Valley of Mexico

60 STANDING FIGURE IN SERPENTINE
Aztec culture. Valley of Mexico

61 SERPENTINE MASK
Tarascan culture. Guerrero, Mexico

62 STONE MASK SHOWING TATTOOING
Totonac culture. Vera Cruz, Mexico

*63 LARGE CARVED SERPENTINE FIGURE SHOWING TATTOOING ON BODY
Totonac (?) culture. Vera Cruz, Mexico

64 STONE FACADE ORNAMENT WITH MONKEY AND HUMAN HEAD IN JAW OF BIRD
Totonac culture. Vera Cruz, Mexico

65 CALCITE BOWL IN FORM OF RABBIT
Totonac culture. Island of Sacrifice, Vera Cruz, Mexico

Lent by The University Museum, Philadelphia

*66 STELA NO. 13, PIEDRAS NEGRAS, GUATEMALA
Maya culture. Dated 511 A.D. Eldridge R. Johnson Middle American Expedition, The University Museum, 1931

*67 LINTEL NO. 3, PIEDRAS NEGRAS, GUATEMALA
Maya culture. Shows a Maya ceremony centering around a throne. Eldridge R. Johnson Middle American Expedition, The University Museum, 1931

*68 FIGURE OF SEATED MAN IN BLACK STONE
Quiché culture. Guatemala

69 FIGURE OF CAPTIVE IN BLACK LAVA
Quezaltenango, Guatemala

*70 MARBLE VASE WITH HANDLES IN FORM OF INTERTWINED JAGUARS
Maya culture. Uloa Valley, Honduras

71 MARBLE VASE
Maya culture. Uloa Valley, Honduras

72 MARBLE VASE
Maya culture. Uloa Valley, Honduras

73 STONE HEAD, probably the Goddess Chalchihuitlicue
Probably Aztec culture. Valley of Mexico

74 SMALL STONE MASK
Toltec or Aztec civilization. Mexico

75 MASK OF GREEN STONE WITH WHITE SPOTS SERVING AS EYES
Probably Toltec culture. Mexico

76 SMALL STONE MASK WITH LONG NOSE
Possibly Cohuixca culture. Guerrero, Mexico

77 SMALL MASK OF OBSIDIAN
Aztec or Toltec culture. Mexico

78 LARGE STONE MASK
Aztec or Toltec culture. Mexico

79 MASK OF TRANSLUCENT ONYX
Aztec or Toltec culture. Mexico

*80 MASK OF GREEN STONE WITH PERFORATED EYES, probably the Old Fire God
with jaguar aspect
Totonac culture. Papantla, Vera Cruz, Mexico. Collection of Mrs. Elsie McDougall

81 ONYX VASE WITH MONKEY IN RELIEF
Aztec or Toltec culture. Mexico

82 JADE CARVING
Mexico

83 AXEHEAD MODIFIED INTO HUMAN FORM
Mexico

84 SMALL HUMAN FIGURE OF GREEN STONE
Mexico

85 STONE PROFILE HEAD WITH TENON, probably for insertion in masonry
Totonac culture. Vera Cruz, Mexico. Collection of Mrs. Elsie McDougall

86 STONE FIGURE OF MAN WITH SNAKE ON BACK
Ecuador

*87 STONE EFFIGY BOWL IN FORM OF PUMA OR JAGUAR
Chavin culture. Peru

Lent by the United States National Museum, Washington

88 STONE MASK
Prehistoric. North America

89 SMALL BLACK STONE FIGURE
State of Puebla, Mexico

90 MASK IN ALABASTER
Mexico

*91 SEATED FIGURE IN JADE
Oaxaca, Mexico

92 STONE FIGURE OF WOMAN HOLDING CHILD
Oaxaca, Mexico

93 STONE MASK
Mexico

93A SEATED FIGURE IN DIORITE
Mexico

93B SMALL FIGURE IN TURQUOISE
Huari, Peru

93C SMALL FIGURE IN GREEN STONE
Huari, Peru

93D PUMA IN JADEITE
Peru

93E LLAMA HEAD IN STONE
Cuzco, Peru

94 STONE FIGURE
Toltec culture. Mexico

POTTERY—SCULPTURE AND VESSELS

95 HEAD FROM WHISTLE, in style of the Palenque sculptures
Maya culture. Found near Palenque, Chiapas, Mexico

36

37

111 PORTRAIT HEAD IN RED AND WHITE WARE
Early Chimu culture. Valley of Jequetepeque, north coast of Peru

112 FIGURE JAR IN BLACK WARE
Late Chimu culture. Trujillo, Peru

113 JAR IN RED-ON-BUFF WARE WITH DECORATION OF WARRIORS
Early Chimu culture. Trujillo region, Peru

114 POLYCHROME VASE WITH WARRIOR FIGURES AND SERIES OF MASKS
Early Nazca culture. Peru

Lent by the Museum of the American Indian, Heye Foundation, New York

*115 FIGURE OF MAN HOLDING SPEAR AND MASK
Maya culture. Chacula, Huehuetenango, Guatemala

116 CARVED VASE DECORATED WITH HUMAN FIGURE IN LOW RELIEF
Maya culture. Maxcanu, Yucatan

117 SEATED FIGURE
Tarascan culture. Jalisco, Mexico

118 POLYCHROME VASE
Cholula, Puebla, Mexico

*119 POLYCHROME JAR
Cholula, Puebla, Mexico

120 POLYCHROME JAR REPRESENTING A WOMAN
Early Nazca culture. Peru

*121 POLYCHROME AND INCISED JAR IN FORM OF TIGER
Early Nazca culture. Peru

122 POLYCHROME JAR REPRESENTING A HUMAN FIGURE, WITH BIRD
Early Nazca culture. Peru

123 POLYCHROME BOWL WITH DECORATION REPRESENTING HEADS
Early Nazca culture. Peru

124 POLYCHROME JAR IN FORM OF BIRD
Early Nazca culture. Peru

125 SMALL PAINTED POTTERY MASK
Valley of Mexico

126 SMALL HUMAN HEAD WITH RED PAINTED DECORATION
Valley of Mexico

127 SMALL HUMAN HEAD
Oaxaca, Mexico

128 SMALL HUMAN HEAD
Oaxaca, Mexico

Lent by the Peabody Museum of Harvard University, Cambridge, Massachusetts

*129 BLACK COVERED DISH WITH JAGUAR HEAD HANDLE
Maya culture. Holmul III, Guatemala. *About 475 A.D.*

130 POLYCHROME COVERED DISH WITH PARROT HEAD HANDLE
Maya culture. Holmul III, Guatemala. *About 475 A.D.*

131 BLACK COVERED DISH
Maya culture. Holmul III, Guatemala. *About 475 A.D.*

*132 POLYCHROME VASE WITH QUETZAL DECORATION
Maya culture. From Tomb 2, Copan, Honduras

*133 TERRA COTTA FIGURINE OF GODDESS WITH WORSHIPPER RESTING IN
LAP
Maya culture. Guatemala

134 HEAD OF FIGURINE WITH HEADDRESS
Maya culture. Jonuta, Chiapas, Mexico

135 THREE HEADS FROM FIGURINES
Uloa Valley, Honduras

136 VASE
Cocle culture. Panama. *Probably late thirteenth century*

Lent by The University Museum, Philadelphia

137 FIGURINE WHISTLE REPRESENTING WARRIOR WITH CAPTIVE
Maya culture. Chipal, Guatemala

39

138 POLYCHROME VASE WITH DECORATION SHOWING SEATED PRIESTS ENGAGED IN CEREMONY
Maya culture. Chamá, Guatemala

*139 POLYCHROME VASE WITH DECORATION SHOWING NOBLE ON JOURNEY WITH BEARERS, SERVANTS AND DOG
Maya culture. Ratinlixul, Guatemala

140 POLYCHROME VASE WITH DECORATION OF FIGURES WITH WANDS, GLYPHS AND ORNAMENTS
Maya culture. Huehuetenango, Guatemala

141 POLYCHROME TRIPOD VASE
Maya culture. Guatemala

142 VASE OF RED WARE WITH CARVED OR STAMPED DECORATION OF HUMAN FIGURES
Maya culture. Majada, Guatemala

143 POLYCHROME BOWL
Maya culture. Benque Viejo, British Honduras. Collection of Percy C. Madeira, Jr.

144 VASE OF LEAD-GLAZE RED AND BLACK WARE WITH DECORATION IN HIGH RELIEF OF WARRIOR IN EAGLE MASK
Maya culture. Chipal, Guatemala

*145 POLYCHROME TRIPOD BOWL OF NICOYA WARE
Probably Alta Gracia, Ometepe Island, Nicaragua

146 SOLID POTTERY FIGURINE OF WOMAN WITH INCISED DECORATION PROBABLY DEPICTING TATTOOING OR BODY PAINTING
Archaic culture. Valley of Mexico

147 FIGURINE WITH LEGS MODIFIED INTO RATTLES
Archaic Zapotec culture. Yanhuitlan, Nochistlan, Oaxaca, Mexico

148 LARGE FIGURINE
Archaic Zapotec culture. Mitla, Oaxaca, Mexico

*149 FUNERARY URN, FIGURE SEATED CROSSLEGGED
Zapotec culture. Cuilapan near Zaachila, Oaxaca, Mexico

*150 FUNERARY URN, YOUNG CHIEF WITH FISH IN HAND
Zapotec culture. Zaachila, Oaxaca, Mexico

151 FUNERARY URN, FIGURE SEATED CROSSLEGGED
Zapotec culture. Near Tlacolula, Oaxaca, Mexico

152 FUNERARY URN, FIGURE SEATED CROSSLEGGED WEARING PECCARY HEAD AS HELMET
Zapotec culture. Miahuatlan, Oaxaca, Mexico

153 FUNERARY URN, STANDING WARRIOR
Zapotec culture. Village of Tanexpa, Oaxaca, Mexico

154 LARGE FIGURINE, PROBABLY WARRIOR WITH WEAPON AND SHIELD
Tarascan culture. Ixtlan, Nayarit, Mexico

155 FIGURINE OF WOMAN
Tarascan civilization. West coast of Mexico

156 TOBACCO PIPE WITH FIGURE OF SEATED MAN
Probably Aztec culture. Mexico

157 LARGE HUMAN HEAD
Teotitlan del Camino, Oaxaca, Mexico

158 SMALL HEAD OF THE OLD FIRE GOD WITH TATTOOED FACE, USED AS A RATTLE
Yanhuitlan, Nochistlan, Oaxaca, Mexico

*159 POLYCHROME VASE CUP SHOWING JAGUAR FIGURES AND HEADS
Tiahuanaco II culture. Peru

160 PAINTED VASE, HUMAN HEAD WITH COIFFURE
Chimu culture. Peru

161 PAINTED VASE, FIGURE OF FROG
Chimu culture. Peru

162 POLYCHROME VESSEL WITH DEMONIACAL CAT-GOD
Early Nazca culture. Peru

163 POLYCHROME VESSEL WITH FIGURES OF BIRDS AND FRUITS
Early Nazca culture. Peru

164 POLYCHROME VESSEL WITH DEMONIACAL CENTIPEDE-GOD ON ONE SIDE AND HUMAN FACES ON OTHER
Early Nazca culture. Peru

165 POLYCHROME VESSEL, FIGURE OF WOMAN
Early Nazca culture. Peru

166 POLYCHROME VESSEL WITH DESIGN OF HUMMINGBIRDS
Early Nazca culture. Peru

167 POLYCHROME VESSEL WITH DESIGN OF DEMONIACAL CAT-GOD
Early Nazca culture. Peru

168 POLYCHROME BOWL WITH DESIGN OF BIRDS
Early Nazca culture. Peru

169 SMALL ARYBALLUS
Inca culture. Peru

Lent by The Brummer Gallery, New York

170 POLYCHROME VESSEL IN FORM OF HEAD
Paracas, Peru

171 POTTERY VESSEL
Peru

172 POTTERY VESSEL
Peru

173 POTTERY VESSEL
Peru

174 POTTERY VESSEL
Peru

175 POTTERY VESSEL
Peru

GOLD AND SILVER

Lent by the American Museum of Natural History, New York

176 LLAMA IN SILVER
Inca culture. Island of Titicaca

*177 LLAMA IN SILVER
Inca culture. Island of Titicaca

178 SILVER FIGURE OF WOMAN
Inca culture. Island of Coati

179 SILVER FIGURE WITH GOLD BANDS
Inca culture. Cuzco, Peru

180 SILVER FIGURE
Inca culture. Cuzco, Peru

Lent by the Peabody Museum of Harvard University, Cambridge, Massachusetts

181 AMULET IN HUMAN FORM
Gold with copper base. *Cocle culture.* Panama. *Late thirteenth century*

182 GROTESQUE AMULET OF GOLD
Cocle culture. Panama. *Late thirteenth century*

183 GOLD AMULET IN HUMAN FORM
Cocle culture. Panama. *Late thirteenth century*

Lent by The University Museum, Philadelphia

*184 CUP OF THIN GOLD WITH HUMAN FACE IN HIGH RELIEF
Repoussé technique. *Chimu culture.* Peru

*185 CUP OF THIN GOLD WITH HUMAN FACE IN HIGH RELIEF
Repoussé technique. *Chimu culture.* Peru

*186 BRONZE KNIFE WITH GOLD BIRD ON HANDLE
Technique of casting. *Inca culture* (?)

*187 PLAQUE OF THIN GOLD WITH FIGURE OF JAGUAR
Repoussé technique. Ecuador

188 PLAQUE OF THIN GOLD WITH HUMAN HEADS AND IN CENTER HEAD OF
JAGUAR WITH NOSE PLUG
Repoussé technique. Ecuador

189 HUMAN FIGURE IN GOLD
Wire technique. From sacred lake of Guatavita. *Chibcha culture.* Colombia

190 HUMAN FIGURE IN GOLD
Wire technique. From sacred lake of Guatavita. *Chibcha culture.* Colombia

43

191 HUMAN FIGURE IN GOLD
Wire technique. From sacred lake of Guatavita. *Chibcha culture.* Colombia

192 HUMAN FIGURE IN GOLD
Wire technique. From sacred lake of Guatavita. *Chibcha culture.* Colombia

193 HUMAN FIGURE IN GOLD
Wire technique. From sacred lake of Guatavita. *Chibcha culture.* Colombia

194 RING WITH HUMAN FACE IN CENTER
From sacred lake of Guatavita. *Chibcha culture.* Colombia

195 FLAT GOLD ORNAMENT WITH STYLIZED HUMAN FIGURE, possibly bat-god
Technique of casting. *Quimbaya culture.* Colombia

*196 FLAT GOLD ORNAMENT WITH STYLIZED HUMAN FIGURE, possibly bat-god
Technique of casting. *Quimbaya culture.* Colombia

197 IDOL OF GOLD HOLDING FLOWERS
Technique of casting. Probably a container. *Quimbaya culture.* Colombia

*198 IDOL OF GOLD HOLDING FLOWERS
Technique of casting. Probably a container. *Quimbaya culture.* Colombia

*199 GOLD DISK WITH STYLIZED HUMAN FACE
Repoussé technique. *Quimbaya culture.* Colombia

200 GOLD DISK WITH STYLIZED HUMAN FACE
Repoussé technique. *Quimbaya culture.* Colombia

201 GOLD STAFF HEAD IN FORM OF BIRD
Quimbaya culture. From near Ayapel, Antioquia, Colombia

202 GOLD PENDANT IN FORM OF EAGLE
Technique of casting. Costa Rica

203 GOLD PENDANT IN FORM OF JAGUAR OR MONKEY
Hammered technique. Costa Rica

204 GOLD PENDANT IN FORM OF EAGLE
Technique of casting. Costa Rica

205 GOLD PENDANT IN FORM OF JAGUAR
Technique of casting. Costa Rica

206 GOLD PENDANT IN FORM OF MONKEY
Technique of casting. Costa Rica

207 GOLD BELL IN FORM OF MONKEY SEATED ON TWISTED GOLD ROPE
Technique of casting. Costa Rica

Lent by Alfred M. Tozzer, Cambridge, Massachusetts

208 POTTERY BOWL COVERED WITH GOLD
Veraguas culture. Panama. *Late thirteenth century*

Lent by The Brummer Gallery, New York

209 GILDED SILVER FIGURINE
Peru

210 GILDED SILVER FIGURINE
Peru

211 PAINTER'S PALETTE IN GOLD WITH ENGRAVED HANDLE
Peru

212 BRONZE FIGURE, ANIMAL WITH HUMAN HEAD
Peru

213 BRONZE MASK
Chancay, Peru

214 SILVER IDOL
Corong, Northern Peru

215 BRONZE FIGURE
Peru

216 BRONZE FIGURE
Peru

TEXTILES

Lent by the American Museum of Natural History, New York

217 HEADDRESS OF FEATHER MOSAIC
Late Chimu culture. Peru. Collection of George D. Pratt

45

218 TAPESTRY WITH DESIGN OF GODS AND CATS
Late coast type, probably Pachacamac. Peru

219 FRAGMENT OF TAPESTRY
Tiahuanaco II style. Possibly from Pachacamac. Peru

220 FIGURE OF A GOD, CUT FROM TAPESTRY
Probably from Pachacamac. Peru

Lent by The Metropolitan Museum of Art, New York

*221 FRAGMENT, probably of a garment
Cotton embroidered in wool. *Highlands, Tiahuanaco II culture. Peru. About 600 A.D.*

*222 FRAGMENT, probably of a shirt
Tapestry-woven in wool (cotton warp). *Highlands, Tiahuanaco II culture. About 800 A.D.*

223 SLEEVELESS SHIRT
Tapestry-woven in wool. *Highlands, period of decline of Tiahuanaco II culture. Peru. Tenth century A.D.*

*224 FRAGMENT, possibly of a garment
Tapestry-woven in wool (cotton warp). *Coast, Late Chimu culture. Peru. Eleventh century A.D.*

Lent by Herman A. Elsberg, New York

*225 HALF OF TUNIC IN FEATHER MOSAIC
Early Nazca with Tiahuanaco II influence. Peru. About 600 A.D.

*226 EMBROIDERY ON A CONCEALED BASE-FABRIC
Early Nazca period. Peru. 400-600 A.D.

227 TUNIC OF WOOL-ON-COTTON TAPESTRY
Tiahuanaco II period. Peru. 800-850 A.D.

228 FRAGMENT OF TAPESTRY WITH SLITS
Late Chimu period. Peru. Tenth century A.D.

229 PANEL OF TAPESTRY WITH SLITS
Beginning of late Chimu period. Peru. Early tenth century A.D.

230 FRAGMENT OF TAPESTRY WITH SLITS
Chimu period. Peru. First half of tenth century A.D.

Lent by the Museum of Fine Arts, Boston, Massachusetts

231 WOOL FABRIC EMBROIDERED WITH DECORATION OF ROWS OF DANCERS
Early Nazca culture. Peru. Probably 100–600 A.D.

232 PAINTED COTTON FABRIC WITH PATTERN OF MEN
Late Chimu culture. Peru. 900–1400 A.D.

233 DOUBLE CLOTH WITH DESIGN OF CONVENTIONALIZED FISH AND BIRDS
Late Chimu culture. Peru. 900–1400 A.D.

CONTEMPORARIES

BEN BENN

234 MAN AND MOUNTAINS, *oil, 1917*
Collection Gallery 144 West 13th Street, New York

235 MASK AND SUN, *watercolor, 1917*
Collection Gallery 144 West 13th Street, New York

JEAN CHARLOT

236 LA TORTILLERA, *oil, 1929*
Collection the Artist

237 MOTHER AND CHILD, *oil*
Collection Alfred H. Barr, Jr., New York

238 THE BUILDERS, *oil*
Private Collection, New York

239 BATHER, *watercolor*
Collection Miss Anita Brenner, *New York*

240 COPY OF FRESCO, Chichen Itza
Collection Carnegie Institution of Washington

JOHN FLANNAGAN

241 SERPENT, *stone, 1930*
Collection Weyhe Gallery, *New York*

242 NUDE, *stone, 1930*
Collection Weyhe Gallery, *New York*

RAOUL HAGUE

243 GIRL WITH FUR, *stone, 1931*
Collection the Artist

244 FIGURE, *stone, 1931*
Collection the Artist

CARLOS MERIDA

245 THE RIVER, *watercolor, 1927*
Collection Delphic Studios, *New York*

246 TROPICO, *watercolor, 1929*
Collection Delphic Studios, *New York*

247 REBAÑO, *oil, 1929*
Collection Delphic Studios, *New York*

ANN A. MORRIS

248 COPY OF FRESCO, Chichen Itza
Collection Carnegie Institution of Washington

DIEGO RIVERA

249 EL ALBA, *watercolor, 1931*
Collection Mr. and Mrs. John A. Dunbar, *New York*

48

250 EL SACRIFICIO, *watercolor*, 1931
Collection Mr. and Mrs. John A. Dunbar, New York

251 LAS PREUBAS DE XIBALBA, *watercolor*, 1931
Collection Mr. and Mrs. John A. Dunbar, New York

DAVID ALFARO SIQUEIROS

252 THE YELL, *oil*
Collection Miss Anita Brenner, New York

253 LA PENITENTERIA, *oil*, 1929
Collection Delphic Studios, New York

254 MASK, *oil*, 1930
Collection Weyhe Gallery, New York

255 SEATED BATHER, *oil*, 1930
Collection Weyhe Gallery, New York

MARION WALTON

256 FAMILY, *stone*, 1932
Collection Weyhe Gallery, New York

257 ALONE, *wood*, 1932
Collection Weyhe Gallery, New York

MAX WEBER

258 NUDE WITH FLOWER, *pastel*, 1911
Collection the Artist

259 REPOSE, *oil*, 1921
Collection the Artist

260 TRANQUILITY, *oil*, 1930
Collection The Downtown Gallery, New York

261 THREE FIGURES, *charcoal drawing*, 1910
Collection The Downtown Gallery, New York

HAROLD WESTON

262 NIGHT, *oil*, 1927
   Collection the Artist

263 SLEEP, *oil*, 1933
   Collection the Artist

WILLIAM ZORACH

264 RABBIT, *stone*, 1930
   Collection Whitney Museum of American Art, New York

265 CAT, *stone*, 1930
   Private Collection, New York

266 SEATED CHILD, *stone*, 1929
   Collection The Downtown Gallery, New York

PLATES

37 HEAD OF MAIZE GODDESS IN TRACHYTE
Maya culture. Copan, Honduras. About 515 A.D.
Lent by the Peabody Museum of Harvard University, Cambridge, Massachusetts

4 STONE MASK
Totonac culture. Vera Cruz, Mexico
Lent by the American Museum of Natural History, New York

5 STONE DISK

Totonac culture. Vera Cruz, Mexico

Lent by the American Museum of Natural History, New York

11 SEATED FIGURE
Late Huaxtec culture. Vera Cruz, Mexico
Lent by the American Museum of Natural History, New York

13 STONE FIGURE OF TATTOOED MAN
Guetar culture. Costa Rica
Lent by the American Museum of Natural History, New York

19 FIGURE OF MAIZE GODDESS
Aztec culture. Valley of Mexico
Lent by the American Museum of Natural History, New York

20 GODDESS CHALCHIHUITLICUE
Aztec culture. Valley of Mexico
Lent by the American Museum of Natural History, New York

26 STONE HEAD
Maya culture. Copan, Honduras
Lent by the Museum of the American Indian, Heye Foundation, New York

30 GOD XIPE TOTEC, stone
Aztec culture. Pepepan, Valley of Mexico
Lent by the Museum of the American Indian, Heye Foundation, New York

31 SEATED STONE FIGURE
San Bartolo, Mexico
Lent by the Museum of the American Indian, Heye Foundation, New York

35 STANDING FIGURE, GREEN STONE
Central Mexico
Lent by the Museum of the American Indian, Heye Foundation, New York

36 STONE CARVING, ANIMAL HEAD
Chilanga, Salvador
Lent by the Museum of the American Indian, Heye Foundation, New York

41 SERPENT HEAD IN TRACHYTE
Maya culture. Copan, Honduras. About 525 A.D.
Lent by the Peabody Museum of Harvard University, Cambridge, Massachusetts

67 LINTEL NO. 3, PIEDRAS NEGRAS
Guatemala. *Maya culture*
Lent by The University Museum, Philadelphia

45 LINTEL NO. 2, PIEDRAS NEGRAS
Guatemala. *Maya culture. Dated 398 A.D.*
Lent by the Peabody Museum of Harvard University, Cambridge, Massachusetts

46 PORTION OF LINTEL NO. 1, PIEDRAS NEGRAS
Guatemala. Maya culture. Approximately same date as No. 45
Lent by the Peabody Museum of Harvard University, Cambridge, Massachusetts

43 ROMAN NOSED GOD IN TRACHYTE
Copan, Honduras
Lent by the Peabody Museum of Harvard University, Cambridge, Massachusetts

47 HEAD OF A GOD IN STUCCO
Maya culture. Palenque, Chiapas, Mexico
Lent by the Peabody Museum of Harvard University, Cambridge, Massachusetts

50 JADE AMULET, PIEDRAS NEGRAS TYPE
Maya culture. From Cenote of Sacrifice, Chichen Itza, Yucatan
Lent by the Peabody Museum of Harvard University, Cambridge, Massachusetts

52-57 OBJECTS IN JADE
Maya culture. From Cenote of Sacrifice, Chichen Itza, Yucatan
Lent by the Peabody Museum of Harvard University, Cambridge, Massachusetts

59 JADE MASK REPRESENTING GODDESS COYALXANHIU
Aztec culture. Valley of Mexico
Lent by the Peabody Museum of Harvard University, Cambridge, Massachusetts

66 STELA NO. 13, PIEDRAS NEGRAS
Guatemala. *Maya culture. Dated 511 A.D.*
Lent by The University Museum, Philadelphia

**63 LARGE CARVED SERPENTINE FIGURE SHOWING
TATTOOING ON BODY**
Totonac (?) culture. Vera Cruz, Mexico
Lent by the Peabody Museum of Harvard University, Cambridge, Massachusetts

68 FIGURE IN BLACK STONE
Quiché culture. Guatemala
Lent by The University Museum, Philadelphia

70 MARBLE VASE
Maya culture. Uloa Valley, Honduras
Lent by The University Museum, Philadelphia

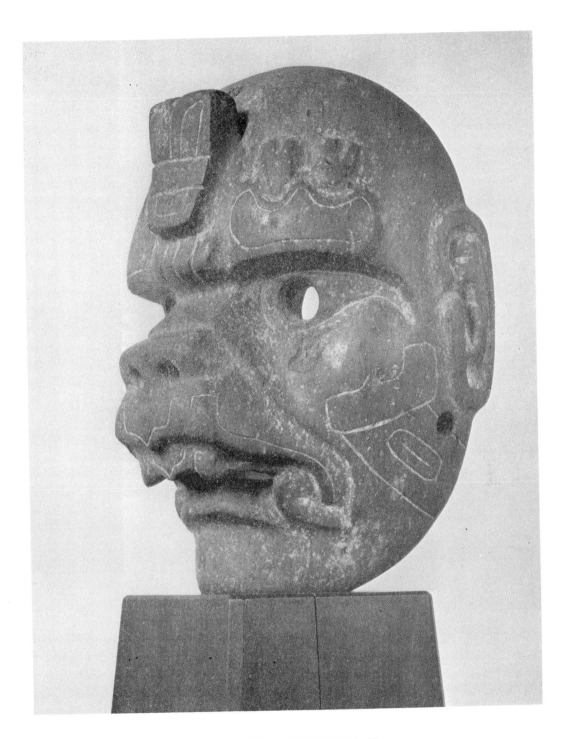

80 MASK IN GREEN STONE
Totonac culture. Papantla, Vera Cruz, Mexico
Lent by The University Museum, Philadelphia

87 STONE EFFIGY BOWL IN FORM OF JAGUAR
Chavin culture. Peru
Lent by The University Museum, Philadelphia

21 DRUM OF WOOD
Aztec culture. Valley of Mexico
Lent by the American Museum of Natural History, New York

91 JADE FIGURE
Oaxaca, Mexico
Lent by The Brummer Gallery, New York

100 LAUGHING HEAD IN CLAY
Totonac culture. Vera Cruz, Mexico
Lent by the American Museum of Natural History, New York

103 FIGURE OF WOMAN IN CLAY
Tarascan (?) culture. Ixtlan, Nayarit, Mexico
Lent by the American Museum of Natural History, New York

105 BLACK POTTERY BOWL
Tarascan (?) culture. Chupicuaro, Guanajuato, Mexico
Lent by the American Museum of Natural History, New York

115 FIGURE OF MAN HOLDING SPEAR AND MASK
Maya culture. Chacula, Huehuetenango, Guatemala
Lent by the Museum of the American Indian, Heye Foundation, New York

129 COVER OF BLACK POTTERY BOWL
Maya culture. Holmul III, Guatemala. About 475 A.D.
Lent by the Peabody Museum of Harvard University, Cambridge, Massachusetts

132 POLYCHROME VASE
Maya culture. Copan, Honduras
Lent by the Peabody Museum of Harvard University, Cambridge, Massachusetts

133 GODDESS WITH WORSHIPPER RESTING IN LAP
Terra cotta. *Maya culture.* Campeche, Mexico
Lent by the Peabody Museum of Harvard University, Cambridge, Massachusetts

139 POLYCHROME VASE SHOWING NOBLE ON A JOURNEY
Maya culture. Ratinlixul, Guatemala
Lent by The University Museum, Philadelphia

145 POLYCHROME TRIPOD BOWL, NICOYA WARE
Probably Alta Gracia, Ometepe Island, Nicaragua
Lent by The University Museum, Philadelphia

149 FUNERARY URN
Zapotec culture. Cuilapan, Oaxaca, Mexico
Lent by The University Museum, Philadelphia

150 FUNERARY URN
Zapotec culture. Zaachila, Oaxaca, Mexico
Lent by The University Museum, Philadelphia

159 POLYCHROME VASE CUP SHOWING JAGUAR FIGURES
AND HEADS
Tiahuanaca II culture. Peru
Lent by The University Museum, Philadelphia

119 POLYCHROME JAR
Cholula, Puebla, Mexico
Lent by the Museum of the American Indian, Heye Foundation, New York

121 POLYCHROME AND INCISED JAR
IN FORM OF TIGER
Early Nazca culture. Peru
*Lent by the Museum of the American Indian,
Heye Foundation, New York*

177 LLAMA IN SILVER
Inca culture. Island of Titicaca
Lent by the American Museum of Natural History, New York

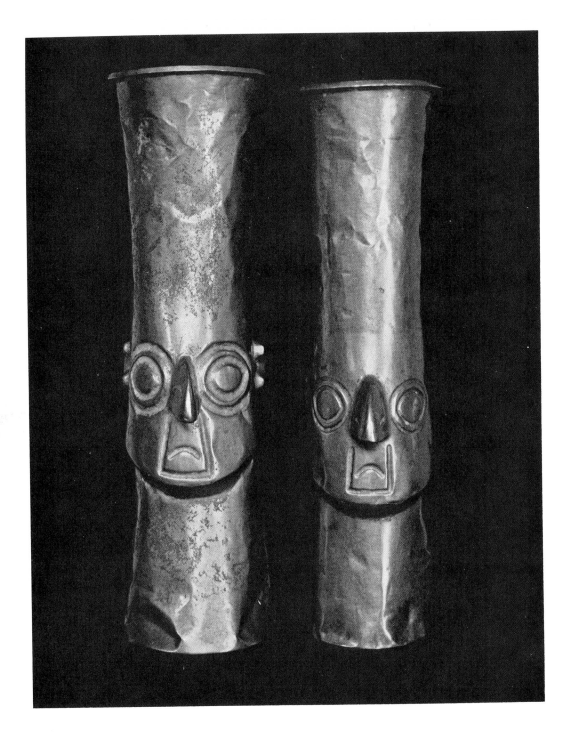

184–185 CUPS OF THIN GOLD WITH HUMAN FACE IN HIGH RELIEF
Repoussé technique. *Chimu culture.* Peru
Lent by The University Museum, Philadelphia

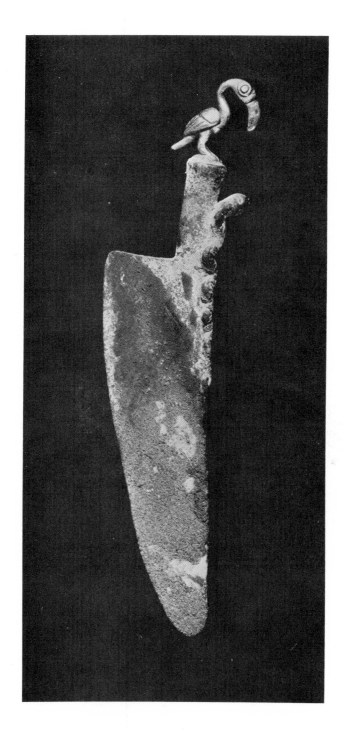

186 BRONZE KNIFE WITH GOLD BIRD ON HANDLE
Technique of casting. *Inca culture* (?)
Lent by The University Museum, Philadelphia

196 FLAT GOLD ORNAMENT WITH STYLIZED HUMAN FIGURE,
POSSIBLY BAT-GOD
Technique of casting. *Quimbaya culture.* Colombia
Lent by The University Museum, Philadelphia

187 PLAQUE OF THIN GOLD WITH FIGURE OF JAGUAR
Repoussé technique. Ecuador
Lent by The University Museum, Philadelphia

199 GOLD DISK WITH STYLIZED HUMAN FACE
Repoussé technique. *Quimbaya culture.* Colombia
Lent by The University Museum, Philadelphia

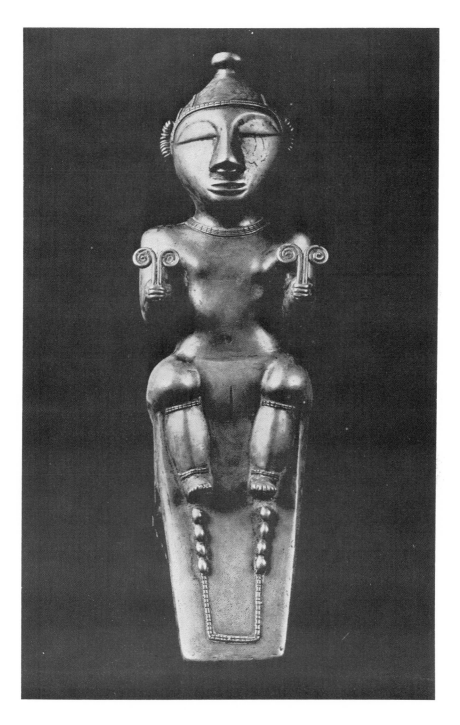

198 IDOL OF GOLD HOLDING FLOWERS
Technique of casting. *Quimbaya culture.* Colombia
Lent by The University Museum, Philadelphia

222 FRAGMENT, PROBABLY OF A SHIRT
Highlands, Tiahuanaco II culture. About 800 A.D.
Lent by The Metropolitan Museum of Art, New York

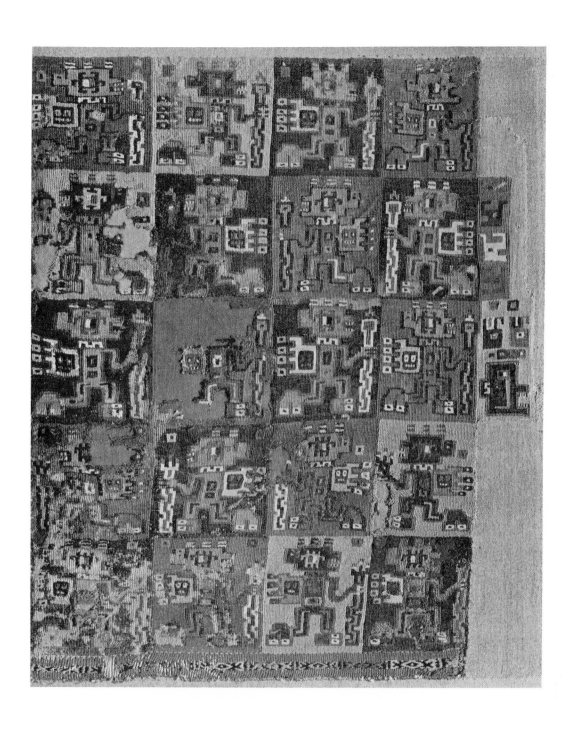

221 FRAGMENT OF TAPESTRY IN WOOL (COTTON WARP)
Late Chimu culture. Peru. Eleventh century A.D.
Lent by The Metropolitan Museum of Art, New York

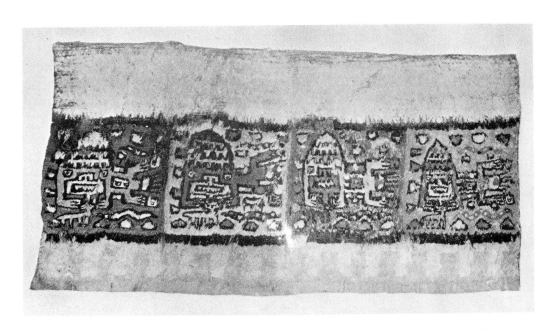

225 HALF A TUNIC IN FEATHER MOSAIC
Early Nazca with Tiahuanaco II influence. Peru. About 600 A.D.
Lent by Herman A. Elsberg, New York

226 EMBROIDERY ON CONCEALED BASE-FABRIC
Early Nazca culture. Peru. 400–600 A.D.
Lent by Herman A. Elsberg, New York

224 FRAGMENT, POSSIBLY OF A GARMENT
Coast, Late Chimu culture. Peru. Eleventh century A.D.
Lent by The Metropolitan Museum of Art, New York

TWENTY-FIVE HUNDRED COPIES OF THIS CATALOG
WERE PRINTED FOR THE TRUSTEES OF THE MUSEUM
OF MODERN ART, NEW YORK, BY THE GARRETT
PRESS, NEW YORK, MAY, NINETEEN THIRTY-THREE